THOREAU & ME
IN THE FINGER LAKES

Books by
MARK W. HOLDREN

Spirit Wolf

The Raven

Lost Pond

Back Roads of the Finger Lakes

Thoreau & Me in the Finger Lakes

THOREAU & ME
IN THE FINGER LAKES

by
MARK W. HOLDREN

∽

Powell Hill Press
Penfield, NY

www.powellhillpress.com

Copyright 2016
by Mark W. Holdren

All rights reserved. No part of this book may be reproduced, stored in a retrieval system or transmitted by any means, electronic or otherwise, without permission from the author.

ISBN 978-0-9760648-4-8

Powell Hill Press
PO Box 992
Penfield, NY 14526
www.powellhillpress.com

Cover Design by
Brancato Creative

Illustrations by
Elaine Verstraete

Cover Photo by
iStock.com/Toltek

Author Photo by
Gary Whelpley

Printed in the United States of America

To
Marie-France

AKNOWLEDGEMENTS

No book is written alone.
The author extends his heartfelt thanks
and gratitude to Marie-France Etienne,
Derek Doeffinger, Elaine Verstraete,
Ron Brancato, Emma Lynge and Linda Reber,
all of whom helped bring
Thoreau & Me in the Finger Lakes
to life.

Part I
THE NATURAL MAN

∽

"A lake is the landscape's most beautiful and expressive feature. It is earth's eye, looking into which the beholder measures the depths of his own nature."

—Henry David Thoreau (HDT), Walden, "The Ponds"

The sun has caught the morning mist, tugging it from the shimmering surface of the lake in ghostly plumes of pastel pink and battleship gray. My kayak slips silently past the shoreline, nudged along by a rising breeze. I lower my hands into the bluestone water and touch the very source of my creation.

At Walden Pond, Henry David Thoreau gazed into "a perfect forest mirror."

What might he have seen this autumn morning at Canadice Lake?

Thoreau defined the art of sauntering while roaming the hills and forests surrounding Concord, Massachusetts. But he was not a frequent traveler. He ventured out of New England only on rare occasions, visiting New York City, and on two more rigorous sojourns to travel to Minnesota and Canada. While he probably traveled as far as his modest means and short life allowed — he died of tuberculosis in his forty-fifth year — there is little he did not see, viewing the world with an open heart and vivid imagination.

Henry David Thoreau never traipsed the Finger Lakes country.

Yet he is with me this morning. I feel his undeniable presence whenever I wish to be one with the land.

"We can never have enough of nature. We must be refreshed by the sight of inexhaustible vigor…the wilderness…the thunderclouds…the rain…"

—HDT, *Walden*, "The Spring"

He is at my side when I eagerly don coat and boots and wade into a winter blizzard, "staggering blind through the storm-whirl," as Robert Service wrote, all the while wondering why my neighbors haven't joined me for such a glorious evening trek down an unplowed country road. He nods approvingly when I find pleasure paddling the West River in a summer rain, joy in the roar of the wind through Clark's Gully, and inspiration beneath a storm-torn South Bristol sky.

"*We can never have enough of nature.*"

Now there is scientific evidence that Thoreau was onto something, evidence that helps us better understand the deep-seated connection between humans and the natural world, a bond that is now more essential to our health and well-being than ever before.

Studies show that just several hours spent in natural surroundings can lower concentrations of the stress hormone cortisol, lower blood pressure and heart rate, reduce levels of two more stress-related hormones, (adrenaline and noradrenalin), and increase natural killer cells that help our bodies fight disease.

These studies and others serve as the cornerstones of a form of eco-therapy the Japanese call shinrin-yoku or "forest air breathing," embracing the natural environment with all the human senses — sight, hearing, taste, touch and smell.

Thoreau, unbeknownst to the world more than a century-and-a-half ago, was practicing an early form of shinrin-yoku. "My nerves are steadied, my senses and my mind do their office," he wrote of being immersed in nature.

The breeze has shifted. The kayak is drifting into the center of the lake. And I am floating into a mystical sense of oneness with my surroundings. With hands still wrist-deep in the bracing water, I breathe deeply, and a reassuring sense of peace pours into my being.

Thoreau was onto something indeed.

If it had been his good fortune to have ambled across western New York State, he would surely have written of Canadice Lake, one of those magical places woven into the fabric of the Finger Lakes country — some remote, others hiding in plain sight — where it is possible to connect with nature in remarkably powerful ways, where all the human senses come incredibly alive.

When Thoreau died, his last words were reportedly "moose…Indians." I wonder what he saw. I wonder what he would have seen in the Finger Lakes country.

Who was this *Natural Man*, Henry David Thoreau?

"I am a Schoolmaster — a Private Tutor, a Surveyor — a Gardener — a farmer — a Painter, I mean House Painter, a Carpenter, a Mason, a Day Laborer, a Pencil-Maker, a Glass-paper Maker, a Writer, and sometimes a Poetaster."

—Correspondence, to Henry Williams, Jr.
September 30, 1847

Oliver Wendell Holmes granted Thoreau "many rare and admirable qualities," describing him as a "unique individual, half-college graduate and half-Algonquin, who carried out a schoolboy whim to its full proportions," and a "nullifier of civilizations, who insisted on nibbling his asparagus at the wrong end."

Ralph Waldo Emerson thought his friend, Henry, "sincerity itself, and might fortify the convictions of prophets in the ethical laws by his holy living."

Henry David Thoreau, in short, dedicated his life to the art of living well.

He was born in Concord, Massachusetts, on July 12, 1817, and died there on May 6, 1862. His father was of French Huguenot descent. His mother was Scottish, from whom Thoreau inherited an early love of nature. He had one brother, John, and two sisters, Helen, who died at a young age, and Sophia, who managed her renowned brother's fame long after his death.

Young Henry attended public grammar school and later Concord Academy. He entered Harvard in 1833, which he derisively referred to as "Cambridge College." There he was quickly identified as "one who preferred to go his own way." At Harvard, Thoreau discovered Emerson's seminal essay, Nature. It would become a major influence on his life. Nature defined New England Transcendentalism, through which Thoreau further strengthened his reverence of all things wild. It also nurtured his belief that nature could bring out the very best in him — the very faith that would find him some eight years later living alone in a crude hut on the shores of Walden Pond.

A friend, Ellery Channing, described Thoreau:

In height, he was about average (he himself says about five foot, seven inches); in his build, spare, with limbs that were rather longer than usual...His face, once seen, could not be forgotten. The features were quite marked: the nose aquiline or very Roman...more like a beak; large overhanging brows over the deepest set of blue eyes that could be seen...The mouth with prominent lips, pursed up and meaning and thought when silent, and giving out when open a stream of the most varied and unusual and instructive sayings. His hair (which he parted on the left side) was a dark brown, exceedingly abundant, fine and soft. His whole figure had an active earnestness, as if he had no moment to waste. The clenched hand betokened purpose.

Another acquaintance said Thoreau's posture was so erect it seemed "impossible that he could ever lounge or slouch." Another said his arms were covered with thick dark hair, "like a pelt."

After graduating from Harvard in 1837, Thoreau taught briefly at Concord's public school. He also began, at Emerson's urging, the first of thousands of entries that would compose his famed journal. Thoreau quickly abandoned public education, however, when he learned he was required to flog his students. He and his brother then opened a private school. Nature studies were an important part of Thoreau's curriculum. He believed some of his own best learning had been acquired in the out-of-doors.

While his immediate vocation was teaching, Thoreau's heart was in writing and lecturing. He believed making a name for himself in the "lecture field" would speed his entry into print. Almost every town had its lyceum, its pine stages mounted weekly by the great as well as the soon to be forgotten. Thoreau did not immediately succeed as a lecturer. His delivery was called indifferent at best. What his lyceum appearances did do was form the basic style of his writing, informative and aimed directly at the reader. Many of these early lectures also served as the building blocks for some of his most powerful essays on nature.

It was during this time that he and his brother explored the Concord and Merrimack Rivers. Here Thoreau gathered material for what a decade later would be his first published book, *A Week on the Concord and Merrimack Rivers* (1849).

As Thoreau's earnings as a lecturer were meager, he gladly accepted an invitation to take up residence in Emerson's home. There he served as a handyman and gardener. He also became attracted to Emerson's wife, Lydia, but there is no evidence of an affair. While living there, *The Transcendentalist Dial* published nine of Thoreau's poems and his classic essay on nature, "A Natural History of Massachusetts" (1842):

> Men tire of me when I am not constantly greeted and refreshed as by the flux of sparkling streams. Surely joy is the condition of life. Think of the young fry that leap in ponds, the myriad of insects ushered into being on a summer evening, the incessant note of the hyla with which the woods ring in spring, the nonchalance of the butterfly carrying accident and change painted in thousands of hues upon its wing, or the brook trout minnow stoutly stemming the current, the luster of those scales, work bright by attrition, is reflected upon the bank!

After having lived in Emerson's home for two years, Thoreau left in 1843 for Staten Island. There he would tutor Emerson's nephew while promoting his work to the New York literary market. He would also help edit the *Dial*, which would publish more of his essays and poems. It was during this period that his family began to ask what his career path might be and how he would support himself. Thoreau thus declared in his journal that he would live as a poet, a calling he saw nobler than that of the scientist or philosopher. To do so, however, he knew he must reduce his wants and live as simply as possible. Emerson owned land adjacent to Walden Pond, about a mile outside Concord. He offered its use to Thoreau, who, in the spring of 1845, began construction of a tiny, one room cabin. Its cost would be under thirty dollars. Henry David Thoreau moved to Walden Pond on the Fourth of July, 1845.

"I went to the woods because I wished to live deliberately, to front only on the essential facts of life, and see if I could not learn what it had to teach, and not, when I came to die, discover that I had not lived."

— HDT, *Walden*, "Where I lived."

The two years and two months he would spend at Walden Pond would be the most productive years of his

Mark W. Holdren

life. Thoreau believed his well-being required at least four hours a day in the open air. When he wasn't hoeing beans, baking bread or chopping wood, he was walking, sometimes up to twenty miles a day, occasionally staying out all night, "sauntering through the woods and over hills and fields, absolutely free from all worldly engagements."

And he was writing, completing the first draft of *A Week on the Concord and Merrimack Rivers*. It was a scholarly work, awash in transcendental philosophy. Though a publishing failure, it is recognized today as a unique American achievement.

While Thoreau entertained occasional guests at Walden Pond, much of his time was spent alone.

"I have never felt lonesome, or in the least oppressed by a sense of solitude, but once, and that was a few weeks after I came to the woods, when, for an hour, I doubted if the near neighborhood of man was not essential to a serene and healthy life. To be alone was something unpleasant. But I was at the same time conscious of a slight insanity in my mood, and seemed to foresee my recovery. In the midst of a gentle rain while these thoughts prevailed, I was suddenly sensible of such sweet and beneficent society in nature, in the very pattering of the drops, and in every sound and sight around my house, an infinite and unaccountable friendliness all at once like an atmosphere sustaining me, as made the fancied advantages of human neighborhood insignificant, and I have never thought of them since. Every little pine needle expanded and swelled with sympathy and befriended me. I was so distinctly made aware of the presence of something kindred to me, even in scenes which we are accustomed to call wild and dreary, and also the nearest of blood to me and humanist was not a person nor a villager, that I thought no place could ever be strange to me again."

—HDT, *Walden*, "Solitude"

At the cabin he also wrote the first draft of the book that would be translated into twelve languages, the book that would inspire millions, *Walden, or, Life in the Woods*.

"Life, who knows what it is, what it does?" he'd asked himself the day he moved into his cabin. Thoreau believed that most men live lives of quiet desperation, but the poet, the writer, and/or the philosopher need not. The two years he spent at Walden Pond convinced Thoreau that by reducing life to its barest essentials it was possible to set one's own standards and live well by them. He left the cabin for good on a hot summer afternoon in 1847. *Walden* would be published seven years later. Sales would be modest, at best. Thoreau would never know the immense impact Walden would have on the world. He would go on to join the abolitionists' fight against slavery, and produce just one more memorable and provocative work, his essay, "Civil Disobedience."

"My life has been the poem I would have writ, But I could not both live and utter it," he wrote in his journal.

Others saw Thoreau's life differently. His friend and mentor, Ralph Waldo Emerson, said at Thoreau's death:

"The country knows not yet, or in the least part, how great a son it has lost. It seems an injury that he should leave in the midst his broken task, which none else can finish — a kind of indignity to so noble a soul, that he should depart out of Nature before yet he has been really shown to his peers for what he is. But he, at least, is content. His soul was made for the noblest society; he had in a short life exhausted the capabilities of this world; wherever there is knowledge, wherever there is virtue, wherever there is beauty, he will find a home."

Future generations would view Henry David Thoreau a pioneer American conservationist as well as one of America's first and finest nature writers. *Walden* is re-printed more than any other American book published before the Civil War. More than one-hundred-fifty years after its publication, *Walden* is a classic masterpiece, forever helping humans understand their relationship to the natural world.

Thoreau's world view was clearly defined through all five of his senses. "I hear beyond the range of sound. I see beyond the range of sight," he wrote in his poem, "Inspiration."

He reveled in the "wild and primitive fragrance" floating from the fronds of a wild fern.

In the Concord River he saw water as "much more fine and sensitive an element than earth." He viewed the moonlight "like a cup of water to a thirsty man."

In "The Maine Woods," Thoreau's senses were on full alert:

"At length we reached an elevation sufficiently bare to afford a view of the summit, still distant and blue, almost as if retreating from us. A torrent, which proved to be the same we had crossed, was seen tumbling down in front, literally from out of the clouds. But this glimpse at our whereabouts was soon lost, and we were buried in the woods again. The wood was chiefly yellow birch, spruce, fir, mountain-ash, or roundwood, as the Maine people call it, and moosewood.

berries, were very abundant, as well as Solomon's seal and mooseberries. Blueberries were distributed along our whole route; and in one place the bushes were drooping with the weight of their fruit, still fresh as ever."

A century-and-a-half ago Thoreau wrote that walking without presence of mind is a missed opportunity to feed the soul and connect to our essential wildness. It is not surprising, therefore, that there are more copies of *Walden* for sale in the bookshops of Tokyo than in New York City. In Japan, where shinrin-yoku is practiced in more than forty officially designated forest therapy centers, Henry David Thoreau still stands tall.

Mark W. Holdren

Part II
NATURE & YOUR BRAIN

∽

"Nature makes no noise. The howling storm, the rustling leaf, the pattering rain are no disturbance; there is an essential and unexplored harmony in them."

—HDT, *"Journal"*

Would Thoreau have taken a cell phone to Walden Pond?

"The silence rings; it is musical and thrills me. A night in which the silence is audible I hear the unspeakable."

—HDT, *"Journal"*

I think not.

Thoreau was nurtured by the simplicity of his life and the silence it provided him. But today we are wired to the world twenty-four seven, showered by an acoustic downpour of unnerving noise. Our brains are infected daily by infotoxins — information of little value and questionable quality.

In the solitude of Walden Pond, Thoreau sensed the coming storm:

> "We are in great haste to construct a magnetic telegraph from Maine to Texas; but Maine and Texas, it may be, have nothing important to communicate...we are eager to tunnel under the Atlantic and bring the Old World some weeks nearer to the New; but perchance the first news that will leak through into the broad flapping American ear will be that Princess Adelaide has the whooping cough."
>
> —HDT, *Walden*

Invasive digital technologies are robbing us of far more than we can possibly imagine. Constantly connected to our smart digital devices, we immerse ourselves in virtual worlds of artificiality that dumb down our very senses. We check e-mails, texts and tweets by the minute.

Opportunities for engagement with the natural world

are lost, depriving an entire generation of a layer of protection against stress. Is it any wonder so many of today's young people are hooked — many for the rest of their lives — on anti-depressants?

It's easier for a pediatrician to prescribe the latest miracle drug for an obsessively compulsive twelve-year-old than it is to encourage him or her to spend more time outdoors.

Big Pharma spends hundreds of millions of dollars advertising the newest "miracle" drugs. Yet the same TV commercials warn us the pills they're pitching could have dangerous side effects, including death. But enlightened voices are beginning to be heard. There is good medicine to be found far from the pharmacy. There is now scientific evidence that connecting to nature is not only beneficial, but essential to good health.

Of course, Thoreau already knew that nature packed a powerful punch in terms of reinvigorating the human body and soul.

"Measure your health by your sympathy with morning and spring. If there is no response in you to the awakening in nature — if the prospect on an early morning walk does not banish sleep, if the warble of the first bluebird does not thrill you — know that the morning and spring of your life are past."

—HDT, *"Journal"*

Immersion in nature has long been an integral part of Chinese medical practice. Its practitioners teach that the same forces that give life to plants can be transferred to humans, thus improving their well being.

The Roman medical writer Cornelius Celsus (ca 25 BC–ca 50) advocated that walking in gardens and exposure to light and water would aid in human healing.

Frederick Law Olmstead, the father of American landscape architecture, wrote in a report on the status of Yosemite National Park in 1865:

> "If we analyze the operation of scenes of beauty upon the mind, and consider the intimate relation of the mind upon the nervous system and the whole physical economy, the action and reaction which constantly occurs between bodily and mental conditions, the reinvigoration which results from such scenes is readily comprehended."

Olmstead, in the same report, wrote that exposure to nature "not only gives pleasure for the time being but increases the subsequent capacity for happiness."

Harvard biologist Edward O. Wilson began to connect the dots in the 1980s when he identified an inborn emotional connection between humans and other living things. Contact with nature, he wrote, shapes how our brains function.

Wilson's theory has been further developed by scores of researchers. Studies at the University of Virginia showed that infants, when exposed to natural threats they have never seen — spiders for example — showed signs of fear. More university research showed that test subjects who viewed both urban and natural scenes preferred the latter.

Roger S. Ulrich, professor of Architecture at the Center for Healthcare Building Research in Sweden, has devoted his life to proving and advocating the therapeutic powers of nature. His studies — using an electroencephalograph (EEG) to measure brain activity, an electrocardiogram (EKG) to monitor heart activity, and electromyography (EMG) to measure muscle tension — offered proof that immersion in nature can be connected to higher levels of serotonin, which is believed to contribute to feelings of happiness, well-being and stress reduction. Subsequent studies in the United States, Taiwan and Japan have supported Ulrich's initial findings.

Japanese cities are among the most crowded in the world. Yet more than sixty percent of Japan is covered by forests. It is not surprising, therefore, that the practice of shinrin-yoku would be born there in 1982. Initially a marketing strategy created to promote enjoyment of Japan's public lands, the practice of shinrin-yoku initiated research that sought to prove the therapeutic powers of nature.

In 1990, researchers at Japan's Chiba University found lower levels of the stress hormone cortisol in hikers who had spent forty minutes in a forest setting compared to those who spent the same forty minutes walking indoors. Further studies by the university's Center for Environmental Health and Field Services detected lower blood pressure levels and reduced pulse rates among the one thousand shinrin-yoku participants that were studied.

Additional experiments, led by Dr. Qing Li, a senior assistant professor at Nippon Medical School in Tokyo and president of the Japanese Society of Forest Medicine, tested the effects of forest bathing on our moods, stress levels and immune systems.

In one study, the Profile of Mood States (POMS) test was used to show that forest bathing trips significantly increased the participants' vigor while lowering levels of anger, anxiety and depression. This led to a recommendation that frequent forest bathing may help decrease the risk of psychosocial, stress-related diseases.

Studies focusing on immune function looked into whether forest bathing increases the activity of people's natural killer (NK) cells, a component of the immune system that fights cancer. In two studies, small groups of men and women respectively were assessed before and after a two-night, three-day forest bathing trip. During the trips the subjects went on three forest walks and stayed in a hotel in a forest setting. Blood tests were taken before and after the trip, revealing a significant boost in NK activity in the subjects in both groups. The increase was observed as long as thirty days after the trip. Follow-up studies showed a significant increase in NK activity was also achieved after a single day trip to a forest, with increases observed for seven days after the trip.

Dr. Li attributes the increase in NK activity partly to breathing in air containing phytoncide (wood essential oils) like a-pinene and limonene, which are antimicrobial compounds emitted from trees to protect them from rotting and insects.

Ulrich's initial studies — and subsequent research that confirmed his findings — found the presence of a single potted plant in a hospital room aids patient healing. Employees in offices with growing plants had lower levels of stress and fewer sick days.

The same health benefits were found where windows provided a view of natural surroundings.

With 75 percent of the world's population expected to be living in urban environments by the mid twenty-first century, green space is essential as a natural buffer against stress. Research in Denmark found that people living just half a mile from a park, beach or lake were found to have higher levels of stress and were generally in poorer health than those living in natural surroundings. Researchers in Japan, the U.S. and Scotland were able to determine that people living in or near green space have healthier lives and longer life spans.

Researchers in California, using functional magnetic resonance imaging (FMRI), have proven that scenic vistas and other natural views stimulate the portion of the brain that controls levels of dopamine. Higher levels of dopamine can lead to a sense of peacefulness and well-being. Recent studies by Dr. Rodney H. Matuoka at the University of Michigan have linked natural views and settings with not only improved academic performance but also with reduced symptoms of attention deficit disorder.

More than a century ago, Harvard psychologist William James identified the difference between voluntary and involuntary attention. Voluntary attention, like work, he wrote, requires a sustained effort, while involuntary attention simply happens when one is interested or excited by something. Sustained periods of voluntary attention can raise stress levels, while periods of involuntary attention can reduce levels of stress.

Subsequent studies by psychologist Stephen Kaplan introduced the concept that natural environments hold our attention involuntarily or with little effort because we are inherently connected to nature, thus interested or fascinated by natural surroundings. Kaplan's cognitive nature theory proposed that immersion in natural settings could negate levels of fatigue and stress.

> "To my senses the dicksonia fern has the most wild and primitive fragrance, quite unalloyed and untamable, such as no human institutions give out — the early morning fragrance of the world, antediluvian, strength and imparting. They who scent it can never faint."
> —HDT, *"Journal"*

Science identifies the aromatic components of plants as phytoncides — substances produced by plants that have an influence on other organisms. Of course, aromatherapy has been practiced for more than four thousand years. The ancient Greeks used aromatic plant extracts for a wide variety of medicinal and dietary purposes.

While we can smell the bouquet of rose or daffodil, a single tree can release a dozen aromatic chemicals that we cannot discern. But because we cannot smell these airborne aromas does not mean our brains are not responding to them. Phytoncides released from trees can lower stress hormones and reduce anxiety. Aromatic plant chemicals can strengthen the body's antitoxin levels. Studies in Japan have linked the smell of cedar wood and Limonene — another common phytoncide of wood — to decreased systolic blood pressure, improved subjective comfort and a relaxed psychological state.

The German naturalist Peter Wohlleben believes that trees are social beings. In his book, *The Hidden Life of Trees*, he writes that trees can count, learn and remember. His studies show that trees can nurse their sick neighbors, and warn each other of danger by sending electrical signals via network of fungi. Wohllben's studies also suggest that trees can keep the stumps of long dead companions alive by feeding them a sugar solution to their roots.

All the while plants are passing along their "good medicine," providing us with oxygen and cleansing the air of harmful chemicals. Trees are particularly adept at practicing this double duty. NASA uses plants to purify the air astronauts breathe, air that is thick with synthetic chemicals. Quite simply, the air in our forests is cleaner and healthier.

Let nothing come between you and the light.

— HDT, *"Journal"*

Natural sunlight plays a vital role in one's immersion into shinrin-yoku, where visual stimulation is linked to the health benefits previously discussed. Our biological clocks tick to the rise and setting of the sun. We function at our fullest in natural sunlight. Our bodies withdraw as the light fades. Darkness signals our brains to fall asleep. Periods of melancholy and depression are common in the winter months in the northern hemisphere where the days are shorter and natural sunlight reduced. Modern medicine calls this condition seasonal affective disorder, or, appropriately, SAD. Sun exposure to the skin is the human race's natural, intended and most effective source of vitamin D. Artificial light, on the other hand, interferes with our natural rhythms, triggering a host of medical problems, including fatigue and attention deficit hyperactivity disorder. Researchers have linked exposure to natural sunlight to the production of serotonin and enhanced levels of concentration.

> Life in us is like water in a river.
>
> — HDT, *Walden*

Water brings all the senses alive. Rushing over a rocky stream, cascading down a mountainside, reflecting a setting sun or autumn moon, quenching our thirst or invigorating our bodies, water has long held a prominent place in our relationship with the natural world.

And there is more to a streamside stroll than meets the eye. Negative ions are charged molecules we cannot see or taste. They are found at their highest level in forests and near flowing water. Levels are also high just after a rainfall. Negative ions have been proven to enhance our health, promoting longer life and improved cognitive performance. Japanese researchers have shown the sound of moving water changes the flow of blood to levels that are associated with relaxation. Rushing water can also combat the symptoms of SAD.

> "I have met with but one or two persons in the course of my life who understood the art of Walking, that is, of taking walks — who had a genius, so to speak, for sauntering, which word is beautifully derived from idle people who roved about the country in the Middle Ages and asked charity, under pretence of going a la Sainte Terre, to the Holy Land, till the children exclaimed 'There goes a Sainte Terrer,' a Saunterer, a Holy Lander. They who never go to the Holy Land in their walks, as they pretend, are indeed mere idlers and vagabonds; but they who do go there

are saunterers in the good sense, such as I mean… for every walk is a sort of crusade, preached by the Peter the Hermit in us to go forth and reconquer this Holy Land from the hands of the infidels."

— HDT, *Excursions*, "Walking"

Walking is an integral part of the shinrin-yoku process. Its benefits to the human body and brain are well-known: an active lifestyle spent preferably outdoors is effective in preventing a host of chronic diseases such as obesity, diabetes, osteoporosis, and cardiovascular disease. Walking also stimulates brain activity. Dr. George Sheehan, an early jogging guru, wrote: "Never trust an idea arrived at sitting down." He was well aware that exercise improves cognitive functioning. And studies indicate that green exercise is more beneficial to human health than hours spent in the gym.

While the forest's impact on our five senses is clear — and the science of shinrin-yoku continues to advance — there are cynics for whom this simple, natural path to wellness is incomprehensible. For them, one psychotherapist wrote: "I recommend many ways for my clients to connect with nature. They report feeling better, reduced anxiety, and reduced depression. I don't care if there is a solid scientific paper out there that will make some cynic happy. This stuff works."

Mark W. Holdren

Part III
COMING INTO AWARENESS

∽

"We need pray for no higher heaven than the pure senses can furnish… Our present senses are but the rudiments of what they are destined to become."

—HDT, *A Week*, "Friday"

Henry David Thoreau would surely have found the Finger Lakes country as inspiring as any he crossed in his short, yet remarkable life. The "land of lakes and legends" stretches nine thousand square miles, easterly from Rochester to Syracuse and southerly to the New York-Pennsylvania border. It encompasses six major lakes — Canandaigua, Keuka, Seneca, Cayuga, Owasco and Skaneateles — and five lesser lakes — Honeoye, Canadice, Hemlock, Conesus and Otisco.

Legend tells us that the lakes were created when the Great Spirit of the Seneca People placed the imprint of his hand upon the land. Geologists tell a less enchanting story. Glaciers scoured the land from north to south. When the ice melted, and the great ice sheet retreated about 15,000 years ago, their deposits dammed parallel valleys, which then filled with both spring and stream water. This glacial scouring also created the rolling hills and spectacular gorges that define the character of the Finger Lakes country today.

Like the glaciers, the Haudenosaunee — *the people who live in the long house* — the Seneca, Cayuga, Onondaga, Oneida and Mohawk people left their indelible mark upon the land.

No one is sure when the Seneca arrived in the Finger Lakes country. Historians do know they were preceded by migrating Algonkian tribes, and possibly among them a mound-building Eskimo people. Some believe the Seneca began migrating into the Finger Lakes from the south in the early 16th century.

Skaneateles is an American Indian name translated as both *beautiful squaw* and *long lake*. Cayuga means *boat landing*, and Keuka *canoe landing*. To the Seneca,

Canandaigua was "the chosen place," Conesus was known as *sheep berries* and Honeoye *finger lying*. The largest and deepest of the Finger Lakes, Seneca, bears the name of the keepers of the western door of the Iroquois Confederacy. The names of many rivers and streams, towns and counties, were inspired by American Indian names: Mohawk, Genesee, Oatka, Chautauqua, Canaseraga, Irondequoit, Cattaraugus, Nunda, Cayuga and Allegany are just a few.

The Seneca's first disastrous encounter with the white man occurred in 1687 when the governor of France's North American holdings, the Marquis de Denonville, led an army of French troops and their Huron allies across Lake Ontario. Marching southward from what is now Irondequoit Bay, Denonville's army destroyed a large Seneca village near the town of Victor — now Ganondagan State Park — as well as several smaller Seneca settlements.

The French attack sparked a later alliance between the Haudenosaunee and the British. That alliance would prove fatal when General of the Army George Washington ordered Major General John Sullivan and a third of the Continental Army to ravage the land of the Haudenosaunee. "The immediate objective," Washington instructed, "is the total destruction of the settlements of the Six Nations."

Spotting Sullivan's advancing troops — what Seneca

scouts called "the long blue snake"— the Seneca abandoned their villages. Sullivan's troops marched unopposed into the Finger Lakes country, burning the empty villages to the ground and laying waste to fields of corn, apple orchards and stored provisions. By the end of the 18th century the once mighty Haudenosaunee were reduced to living on a handful of small Western New York reservations where they were promised "they would never be disturbed."

The people who live in the long house adapted quickly to modern society. But the indelible imprint their ancestors left upon the land makes the practice of shinrin-yoku in the forests of Finger Lakes even more magical.

One of the beauties of forest bathing is its simplicity. Just being there, opening the senses to the murmuring of a stream, a bird's song, or the fragrance or touch of the trees can be enough to benefit from the forest's healing powers.

The Japanese Society of Forest Medicine offers these forest bathing suggestions:

- Make a plan based on your daily physical activity. Do not get tired during forest bathing.
- If you take a whole day it is better to stay in the forest for about four hours and walk about three miles.
- If you are tired, you can rest anywhere and anytime you like.
- If you feel thirsty, drink water or tea anytime you like.

- You can select the forest bathing course based upon your purpose.
- If possible, take a warm bath or hot spring bath after forest bathing.

Of course, always check weather conditions before heading out. Familiarize yourself with the area, taking along a map and compass if needed. Wear appropriate clothing, and bring rain gear, just in case. Always carry plenty of water, energizing snacks and a first aid kit. Make sure someone knows your itinerary and when you plan to return.

And turn off your cell phone!

While the Japanese have designated scores of specific wooded areas in that country as "official" shinrin-yoku forests, I have discovered my own, where nature's embrace comes, well, naturally.

Mark W. Holdren

HIGH TOR

"Each pine is like a great green feather stuck in the ground."

— HDT, *"Journal"*

I see it in the light, sparkling through the trees as if the Great Spirit has just sprinkled a handful of diamonds into the morning mist. I feel it in the seductive call of the wind, wafting softly through boughs of red pine. I hear it in the distant thunder of cascading water high in the canyon above. The mystical power of Clark's Gully is inescapable, yet it is one of the Finger Lakes country's best-kept secrets.

Clark's Gully is part of New York State's High Tor (craggy hill or peak) Wildlife Management Area. It encompasses 1,700 acres of marshland and 3,400 acres of rugged ridges and wooded hills lying mostly easterly of Naples, New York.

Bearing the name of one of the area's pioneer families, Clark's Gully is carved from the eastern slope of South Hill, which the Seneca call Nundawawao — *the great hill*. This is the legendary birthplace of the Seneca people. This is where the earth opened and the first Seneca people stepped into the world. And it is here that Seneca families brought their dead for a period of mourning before taking them to a formal burial site.

I am grateful the trailhead is not clearly marked. Only a small parking area — at the intersection of Sunnyside Road (off Route 245) and West Avenue in the Ontario County Town of Middlesex — suggests that there is more to this steeply wooded hillside than meets the eye.

The climb to the precipice of the waterfall, the gem of Clark's Gully, is a rigorous one. It will take me, a reasonably conditioned hiker, 30–40 minutes, depending upon how many stops I make along the way. From the waterfall it is another 25 minutes or so to the top of the ridge and South Hill Road.

Of course, I could walk down to the falls rather than climbing up.

But where would be the satisfaction in that?

My ascent begins by rock-hopping across a narrow, but fast-flowing stream. Depending upon the season, it can be a roaring torrent or be bone-dry. This is the spring of the year. There is ample water coursing down the mountainside.

Crossing into the woods — a verdant mix of oak, hickory, and red and sugar maple — my eye is drawn to a round stone. It is about the size of a medicine ball. Strangely, it is encircled by half-a-dozen smaller stones. Further along there are more odd rock arrangements, some placed in circles, others in straight lines. This rock garden is not the work of the long-past Seneca. It is more likely the handiwork of a band of spiritualists who reportedly come here. They believe Clark's Gully is a vortex of extraordinary energy. Their placement of the stones mark what they say are energy lines and fields of consciousness of past civilizations where prayer, ritual and meditation have long taken place.

Who am I to doubt them? I have come to Clark's Gully a dozen times. There is no more powerful place to practice shinrin-yoku than here, where the Seneca were so clearly touched by the land.

The route to the falls can begin either by climbing a gentle ridgeline or taking a somewhat shorter, albeit more challenging route — a mostly hand-over-hand climb up a steep, gravel-strewn slope. Both initial routes intersect with the main trail after a couple of hundred yards.

I choose the ridgeline.

The trail is easy to follow. Even so, someone, a winter climber perhaps, has knotted pink plastic ties to some low-hanging branches to mark the way. The footpath is bordered by spring pussytoes. Their flower heads, like tufts of white hair, stand in stark contrast to the mottled brown blanket of dead leaves that carpet the forest floor. These will decay, of course, enriching the soil and providing nutrients to the plants that grow here. There are mayapples, too, a perennial native herb. Sheltered beneath their umbrella-like leaves, each plant will bear just a single white flower with either six or nine petals. The flower's fruit will be edible in early August. About the size of a plum, the fruit can be eaten raw or cooked and made into jellies and jams. The Seneca harvested the mayapple's roots for a cathartic herb which medical science is now studying for its possible anti-cancer properties.

Climbing higher, the incessant barking of a dog in the valley below has thankfully faded away. The north face of the gully is thick with hemlock, while white and red pines dominate in the sun-splashed south rim.

Rat-a-tat-tat. Rat-a-tat-tat.

It can only be the regal pileated woodpecker. I catch a glimpse of its conspicuous red crest as it marches up the side of a dead oak tree. There are wild blueberries here, and arrowwood, too. The Seneca crafted their arrow shafts from its shoots. The arrowwood's fruit is a favorite of the ruffed grouse.

Clambering on, I spy a large acorn. It's jammed into the cavity of a cracked pine root that crosses the trail. What became of the squirrel that cached it here last fall? Has it forgotten the tasty morsel, or did the bushy tail provide sustenance for a hungry red fox?

Further along, the trail is spotted with a coyote's scat. There is ironweed, another vital medicine in the Seneca's pharmacy. Its roots yield an herb that was used to relieve the pain of child birth. Its flowers and fruits are a favorite food of the whitetailed deer. There is buck sign everywhere. The bark on the trunks of several saplings has been rubbed off. It's the whitetail buck's way of polishing its antlers in preparation for battle over mating does. High Tor is a public hunting area. I wonder if the buck who made his mark here survived last fall's hunting season.

The character of the woods suddenly shifts. The forest opens into a sunny grove of shagbark hickory and oak. A yellow-bellied sapsucker darts past me. It's soon drilling away on a hollow oak. Another oak has been recently worked over by a pileated woodpecker, drilling a fresh, fist-sized hole into the south-facing side of the tree. There are several borings from previous years. This oak must be a popular stop.

The trail crosses a small feeder stream and climbs higher. I scurry up a natural staircase comprised of the spreading roots of a nearby white pine. Thank you, Mother Nature, for a helping hand. Spring beauties line the trail. Their purple-pink flowers are another welcome sign of the warming season. A spring Azure butterfly has joined me, landing for a moment on my shoulder. We pass clumps of Solomon's seal and white-flowered saxifrage. The butterfly abandons me for a cluster of bluets. Also known as Quaker Ladies, their pale blue flowers with yellow centers add a new dimension of color to a woods bursting with new life.

A rising wind whispers through an umbrella of pine that shades both sides of the trail. I've reached the halfway point between the trailhead below and South Hill Road which skirts the ridge above. A yellow birch clings precariously to the edge of the gorge. Its octopus-like roots fight for a foothold in the sand and shale. The view is spectacular. The West River snakes its way across the valley floor below.

Renewing my climb toward the falls, a cluster of bluets catches my eye. Moving closer, camera in hand, I almost trample the rarest of finds. The queen of French cuisine is peering at me through the leaf litter, a single morel mushroom. I take a knee and run my fingers over the ridges and pits of her royal honeycombed crown. Are there more of these much sought after delicacies lurking in the leaves? I poke around, but my morel is alone, perhaps missed by the shroomers who surely hunt here. I consider snapping it up to savor with my evening salad, but instead I bury it beneath a handful of leaves. The shroomer may return.

Further up the trail, a giant old growth hemlock reaches out to me. Given that its trunk is three feet or more in diameter, and that hemlocks require 10 years to grow just one inch, this grand tree could be more than two centuries old. The energy that has nurtured its growth since the reign of the Seneca People is incalculable. Can its power invigorate me as well? Tree hugging is not designated as "official" shinrin-yoku practice. I nonetheless wrap my arms around its mighty waist. Is it my imagination, or did I just feel a subtle yet discernible current touch my heart?

Here I am. Where are you?

It's the melodic call of a red-eyed vireo, and there it is! I am lucky to spot it. Vireos spend most of their time high in the tops of trees. They are often heard but seldom seen. But why am I surprised, embraced as I am by this magical hemlock? And this is *the cathedral*, what I have called this mystical glade since my discovering it more than a decade ago. I close my eyes momentarily, and breathing deeply, thank the Creator for sharing so powerful a place with me. The thunder of falling water rumbles through the trees like a fast-approaching storm. The crown jewel of Clark's Gully lies just below me.

But reaching the edge of the waterfall is tricky business. The decline is precipitous and the footing slick on the dry pine needles that carpet the forest floor. The technique here is to slide over the needles as if on skis, making my way from one tree to the next, grabbing a branch here and a tree root there to slow my descent until reaching the bottom of the gorge.

I make it, still standing.

The water flow here, just above the falls, is only a few feet wide and an inch or so deep. But the bed of the creek is mostly shale which is coated with algae. I cautiously test my footing. One slip — I am just inches from the lip of the falls — could be fatal.

It's sixty feet to the bottom.

Taking one small step at a time, I reach the rock ledge on the other side without incident. Now I can sit, and dangling my feet over the edge, watch the water rush by me and thunder into the canyon below.

Once again, I close my eyes and breathe deeply, letting what my companion Thoreau called the subtle magnetism of nature take hold of my heart. The mist swirls around me, taking me to a far distant place.

A Seneca brave emerges from the fog. He is a magnificent fellow, clad in deerskin. He is willowy and hatchet-faced. His skin is the color of sun-washed chestnut. His coal-black hair glistens like glass in the angular light piercing the rim of gorge. He bounds over the stream with the wild grace of a wolf. Then, sitting cross-legged next to me, he closes his eyes and settles into his own sacred space. What questions has he brought for the Great Spirit that surely dwells here? Has this Seneca come to sort out some turning in his life, to seek courage in battle — for wisdom — perhaps, in making a decision that weighs heavily on him? Or has he come like me, like Thoreau, because "our religion is where our love is?"

I lower a hand into the rushing stream. The current swirls through my fingers, driving the icy water over the rim of the falls. In the valley below the sun will begin drawing this water into the clouds. And the wind will take it to a new place where it will rain down once more, to run free over another mountainside.

The cry of a red-tailed hawk jolts me from my daze.
I open my eyes. The Seneca is gone.
I wonder where the wind will carry me.

Mark W. Holdren

"The river is my own highway, the only wild and unfenced part of the world hereabouts."

— HDT, *"Journal"*

Thoreau & Me

Water is the very source of our creation, embracing us in the womb, comprising of up to 75 percent of our adult body mass. When astronomers search for life in other galaxies, the first element they seek is the presence of water. Just as with plants, water can transmit nature's energy to humans, healing our bodies and soothing our souls. Is it then any wonder that we humans overwhelmingly favor water environments over any other in the natural world? Why we are so willing to pay outrageous prices for waterfront property? Because when we are on the water, we are home.

With a single beat of its elegant wings, the great blue heron rises from the blackish water with the grace of a ballerina. This heron is not pleased by my presence. This is our third encounter in perhaps twenty minutes. Having at last had enough of me, it gains altitude over the cattails and disappears into the mist.

I am paddling the West River Marsh, a 1,700-acre wetland that is an integral part of the High Tor Wildlife Management Area. This marsh might long ago have been drained and developed if it were not for the foresight of a Naples farmer named Louis Graff (1915–1980). Graff's property included a portion of the marsh, which he'd hunted, fished and trapped since boyhood. An ardent conservationist, Graff's passion for the marsh was so profound that it was lovingly referred to as *Louie's Place* by friends and neighbors. When developers threatened the marsh in the 1950s, Graff ignored their more lucrative offers and sold his holdings to the State of New York, thus ensuring the land's long-term preservation.

There are two boat launching sites for the marsh, one off Route 21 in Woodville, the other off Route 245, about three miles north of the Village of Naples. Both have ramps and large parking areas.

I put in this morning at a more modest and unmarked fishing access site off Sunnyside Road, a quarter mile or so from the Clark's Gully parking area.

A marsh is defined as "transitional habitat," where the water table is at or near the surface of the land, clearly separating upland and aquatic environments — in this case Canandaigua Lake.

But is the West River wetland a "marsh," or a "swamp"?

Marshes are characterized by soft-stemmed herbaceous plants, such as cattails and pickerelweed, which are clearly thriving here. Swamps, on the other hand, are dominated by woody plants, like red maples and wetland shrubs, of which the West River wetland is also amply stocked.

So which is it?

O-ka-leeeeee! O-ka-leeeeee!

A red-winged blackbird offers a boisterous clue. It's

calling from a thicket of cattails where these convivial birds prefer to both nest and feed. These cattails also fed the Seneca people. Their thriving village once occupied the flatlands at the northern most edge of Naples. The Seneca ground the cattail's rootstock into meal, ate the young shoots like asparagus, and boiled the immature flower spikes as we do corn on the cob.

So this wetland is, by its "official" definition, a marsh.

But wait. There is a budding red maple just off my bow, and sweet pepperbush, too. Both are common in swamp-like terrain.

No matter — marsh or swamp — the West River in spring exudes an energy that is impossible not to feel.

I taste it in the air, an organic jambalaya, stirred to perfection by the sweetness of birth and the stench of death. Wetlands are oxygen-deprived environments. The constant breakdown of organic matter produces hydrogen sulfide, and the aroma of rotting eggs. But the same process reintroduces carbon, oxygen and sulfur — all life-sustaining elements — back into the environment. Wetlands are also greenhouse gas sinks, where methane, twenty times more potent than carbon dioxide, is both produced and stored.

I see it in the warm yellows and lemon greens with which the Creator has brushed his spring canvas.

I hear it the melodious trill of a peeper; the *jug-o-rum* of a bull frog, the *woooooo-eeeeeek* of a wood duck; the soft whistle of a green-winged teal, the distant honk of a northbound Canada goose.

And I surely feel it when one of the season's first mosquitoes deftly pricks my cheek. She may have flown a mile or more from her birthplace, most likely a ditch of stagnant, fetid water, to locate me. A trifle of the blood she withdraws will provide her sustenance. But the bulk of my donation — no more than a drop or two — will feed her production of eggs. I know that my benefactor is a female; males and non-breeding females feed solely on nectar drawn from flowers and sugars, mostly from rotting plants. She escapes the slap of my hand, but she will be dead in less than a month, if all goes well.

Wetlands are among the most productive ecosystems in the natural world. Thoreau thought them "the marrow of the earth."

> "Hope and the future for me are not in lawns and cultivated fields, not in towns and cities but in the imperious and quaking swamps."
>
> —HDT, *Excursions*, "Walking"

In every direction, above and below the water, the sun is

bringing the marsh to life. There is power to this place. It is undeniably charged with spirit. Photosynthesis — the source of energy for nearly all life on earth — converts light energy into chemical energy, which first flows to plant eaters, then to carnivores, and eventually to organisms that consume organic debris. These patterns often intertwine and deviate. Had I brought my fly rod today and dropped a yellow popper into the lily pads nearby, the largemouth bass lurking there would have surely lengthened the marsh's food chain all the way to my dinner table.

Thoreau came to the marsh — "the wildest and richest gardens we have" — for what he termed self-baptism. "When I die," he wrote, "you will find swamp oak water on my heart."

If baptism is the door to the church, our immersion in nature is the gateway to the soul. By stilling our senses and connecting with the natural world, we can begin to know who we truly are.

"When life looks sandy and barren, is reduced to its lowest terms, we have no appetite, and it has no flavor, then let me visit such a swamp as this, deep and impenetrable, while the earth quakes for a rod around you at every step, with its open water where swallows skim and twist."

— HDT, *Journal*

Mark W. Holdren

The West River is born in the town of Gorham, about twelve miles north of the marsh. More a creek than a river, it flows gently and southerly, paralleling a portion of Canandaigua Lake, but separated from it by South Hill. The river and Naples Creek, which flows into the marsh from the south, feed Canandaigua Lake, as do numerous smaller streams that flow to the lake from deep gorges on both the east and west sides of the lake.

After launching at the Sunnyside access and paddling about a mile southwesterly, the river explorer is presented with three choices: bear right, and follow a narrow branch of the river about a mile to the lake, continue a few hundred yards and turn left into the mouth of Naples Creek, or bear right and follow a wider channel to the lake.

By early summer however, both routes to the lake can be so choked with duckweed that it's all but impossible to navigate. Naples Creek can be paddled for a short distance before its channel is blocked by downed trees.

Having begun this morning's journey at the Sunnyside access, I've paddled leisurely to the river's first fork. A muskrat cruises by, the roots of a cattail gripped firmly between its teeth. It is propelled along by its webbed hind feet, its rat-like tail serving as a rudder. Muskrats — Thoreau called them *musquash* — spend most of their life in the water. They can remain submerged for up to twelve minutes. I raise my paddle and watch. Muskrats are not rats at all, but herbivores —plant eaters — that are also known on occasion to savor fish, even a small turtle or two. My musquash shuffles out of the water and climbs onto a mat of cattail reeds and grasses. This is its resting and feeding area. Quite likely it lives in a dome-shaped lodge, probably not far away. Muskrats are not ashamed to take possession of an abandoned beaver lodge, nor are they the least bit hesitant to move in with a beaver family over the winter. And the beavers don't seem to mind it all.

My presence doesn't bother this musquash one bit. Its fine fur is light brown, still wet, and glistens in the sun. Once a much sought after fur bearer, the few muskrats that are trapped today are caught by a vanishing breed of mostly hobbyist trappers. And that's too bad. Muskrats are prolific breeders, capable of birthing up to five litters per year with an average of five kits per litter.

Do the math.

As muskrats feed mainly on the roots of cattails, *eat-outs*, large areas devoid of growth, can occur when too many muskrats inhabit an area. It can take up to 15 years for these ecologically vital areas to regenerate. My musquash looks healthy enough, weighing three pounds or so. If it can avoid a host of predators and the jaws of a trap, it might live up to four years. I take a photo. Its meal finished, it slips back into the water and quickly disappears beneath the blackish surface.

The breeze nudges the kayak's bow. We turn and the wind carries me back upriver, drifting perhaps thirty yards before coming to rest against a hummock of cattails.

I rest my paddle, sit back, and wait.

It takes a minute or two for the disturbance I've created to dissipate. Like dropping a stone into a placid pool, my movement has created concentric waves in the air. Indiscernible to humans, these invisible ripples are like sonic booms to the birds and small mammals whose activities around me have momentarily come to a stop while my presence is assessed.

A minute or two passes, then the low croak of a pickerel frog signals the community that the coast is clear. On cue, a common yellowthroat takes its perch high atop a cattail.

Which-ity...which-ity.

More frequently heard than seen, this masked warbler of the marsh is easily identified by its white head, the black mask over its eyes, and its yellowish-orange breast.

I reach slowly for my camera. But not slow enough. The yellowthroat is off in a flash.

But a painted turtle has caught my eye. It has risen from the duckweed and climbed onto the remains of a rotting willow trunk. The turtle's carapace — the top of its shell — is olive and smooth. The plate seams are trimmed in a greenish-yellow, and the marginal or outer seams are marked with reddish bars.

The painted turtle is the most widespread turtle in North America, and the oldest, having existed for more than 15 million years. They can live up to 60 years. Three more emerge from the water. Their lower shells, mostly yellow, are easily spotted against the gangrene black log. They join the first, who is already basking in the sun.

Among Native Americans, the turtle is among the most sacred of spirit symbols. The Haudenosaunee believed the earth was created when a turtle rose from the sea, thus the expression, *Turtle Island*. The Turtle clan or *Hadinia den* is one of eight major clans or families of the Haudenosaunee. It is believed that a person who chooses a turtle as their symbol is being asked to honor the creative sources within them.

A wood duck drops out of the azure sky. Lowering its wings and banking sharply to its right, it splashes into an opening in the cattails.

Thoreau, paddling the Assabet River, just west of Boston, noted what at first he called "a splendid male summer duck."

Mark W. Holdren

Later he would write:

> "What an ornament to a river to see that glowing gem floating in contact with the waters! As if the hummingbird should recline its ruby throat and its breast upon the water. That duck was all jewels combined, showing different lusters as it turned on the un-rippled elements in various lights, now brilliant gloss, green, now dusky violet, now rich bronze, now the reflections that sleep in the Ruby's grain."
>
> — HDT, *"Journal"*

I focus my binoculars on the duck's crested head. It's a drake — a male. His iridescent green head shimmers like an emerald in the angular rays of the morning sun. He rides high in the water, cocking his glistening crown as he paddles across the pond.

But this handsome fellow is not alone. His mate has emerged from the cattails. Eight fuzzy chicks follow in her wake. Both wood duck sexes have crested heads, white bellies and long tails. The drake's predominantly green head is marked by two white streaks. One extends back from the bill, another from his elliptical red eye. His white throat has two prongs that extend upward toward the back of each eye. The drake's burgundy chest is stippled with white, and is separated from his bronze side by slivers of black and white.

The female's markings are more subdued. Her head and crest are gray while her body is grayish brown. Unlike her mate, she has an elliptical white eye patch. The chicks are mottled gray. Their heads are mostly black. All have large white patches about their eyes.

This drake and hen most likely paired up while wintering in the Carolinas or Florida. Wood ducks are early spring arrivals, returning to their northern breeding areas before ice out. This pair may have been here since early March, when the hen immediately began searching for a suitable nesting site, preferably in the hollow of a dead tree.

The nest needn't be over or even near the water. Wood ducks have been known to nest a mile or more from open water. The tree's cavity or entrance can be as small as four inches across, the nesting area 12–15 inches deep. This hen lined her nest with down feathers plucked from her breast.

Wood ducks may incubate as many as 16 eggs, which take from 28–37 days to hatch. These chicks left the nest almost immediately after they were born. Encouraged by their mother's call, they clawed their way up from inside the dead tree, and then took the plunge, flapping and floating as much as 300 feet to the ground. Mother then led them to the water where they will mature, never returning to the nest.

Wood ducks are one of a few duck species that perch on branches. They are also the most abundant breeding ducks in the eastern United States, often producing two broods in a single year.

Gently dipping my paddle into the water, I ease the kayak forward. I'm fortunate to take a few photos before the drake suddenly bolts off the water.

Ter-we-ee…ter-we-eeee."

The laborious growl of an outboard motor has breached the morning stillness.

The hen and her chicks beat a splashy retreat to the safety of the cattails.

A pontoon boat the girth of a small river barge lumbers past me. Two fishermen, oblivious to their unwelcome intrusion, extend a friendly wave, but leave an oil-laced haze in their wake. Paddling quickly up wind, I find clean air once again, and make my way into the mouth of Naples Creek.

In contrast to the open marsh, Naples Creek passes through a transitional woodland of swamp maples and willows. The rainbow trout that just two months ago spawned in the creek's upper reaches and its tributaries, Grimes, Tannery and Eelpot creeks, have returned to Canandaigua

Lake. The fishermen who flock here the first of April every year to celebrate what my father coined "trout fishing's wildest opening day" are gone as well.

All but one.

I have come to say hello.

Opening Day in Naples was a cherished family tradition. And skipping school to go fishing made it even more special. My brother, Gary, and I began traipsing the banks of Naples Creek with our fish-happy father almost as soon as we could walk. Opening Day was a more raucous affair in the mid 1950's than it is today. Anglers stood elbow-to-elbow at every pool, jostling for the best casting positions, sometimes slashing each other's lines, even exchanging punches over a lost fish. I once saw a man try to kick a fat rainbow out of the creek with his boot. It might snow the first of April, or you could fish in your t-shirt. You never knew. One thing that never changed was the delicious aroma of wood smoke that hung over every pool. It rose from scores of streamside campfires, smoke seasoned to perfection by sizzling bacon, frying eggs and steaming coffee.

Whatever we might have eaten for breakfast, my brother and I couldn't help but want more. So every couple of hours we'd stop by the official weighing station to see what size fish was leading the Rotary Club's fishing derby.

And grab another doughnut.

We fished with trout egg imitations we created from chilled balls of Vaseline. These were clustered in little sacks we made from our mother's old stockings. Later we used chunks of colored sponges to which our father added a drop of anise oil mixed with cod-liver oil. Some years we caught a fish or two, and sometimes we got skunked — the rainbows having already returned to the lake before the start of the season. Everything hinged on the temperature of the water. Warm rains in early March could trigger the spawning run weeks before the season opener.

Lunch was always at the Naples Hotel, where my father and his cohorts held court. While they swigged their Jenny (it was spelled with a J in those days) and Standard Dry, my brother and I over-dosed on popcorn, Cokes and cheeseburgers. The day would end back at the hotel taproom as well. Rochester radio personalities Jack Slattery and George Haefner — who hosted the derby's awards ceremony — always made the Naples Hotel bar their last stop. I don't think they ever paid for a drink.

But nothing lasts forever.

My father went on to write his *Complete Fishing Handbook for New York State's Fabulous Finger Lakes Trout*. It became an instant classic. Now out of print, a copy reportedly sold recently on eBay for over two hundred dollars. Its price at publication in 1962 was $2.95. My father died in 1989. He was seventy-six.

My brother had moved several years earlier to southern California. He tried to get home once a year, either to fish or go deer hunting, another family tradition. When he did make it home he made sure we'd find our way back to the Naples Hotel. By then he was drinking martinis. He never left the bar without dropping 50 bucks on Naples Hotel t-shirts, sweatshirts and hats. Though he lived in tony Newport Beach and traveled often to Hawaii, his affection for Naples remained resolute. He reminded me repeatedly that one day he would live in Naples.

When he died tragically in California — he was just 52 — I brought his ashes home. We made one last call at the Naples Hotel taproom. I ordered a Bombay Sapphire martini for the two of us. It was his favorite, always with three olives.

Then we hiked a hilltop overlooking Naples Creek. I buried his ashes under a majestic maple where he would have a clear view of his favorite fishing pool.

He'll never miss another opening day.

I am on my way to see him now.

"I have my horizon bounded by woods all to myself."

— HDT, *"Journal"*

Mark W. Holdren

Thoreau & Me

While cascading water is the star of Conklin Gully, I find solace among its magnificent trees.

Shinrin-yoku teaches us that the aromatic chemicals released from trees can lower stress hormones, thus reducing levels of anxiety. This good medicine abounds in the diverse forest that embraces the deep chasms and thundering waterfalls of Conklin Gully, also known as Parish Glen, in recognition of the pioneering Parish family that settled in the Naples area in 1789.

I leave my car in a small parking area off Parish Hill Road and head into the woods. (The north/south "blue trail," meandering more than four-and-a-half miles across this steep hillside, can also be accessed from East Hill Road and near the intersection of Parish Hill and Shay Roads).

A gravel roadway, closed to motor vehicles by a gated barrier, rises slowly through a mix of shagbark hickory, beech and black cherry. It is early spring. The trees are not fully leafed out. The sun's rays bathe the forest floor, nourishing the weeping, umbrella-like leaves of the mayapples that thrive in the moist soil. A native perennial, the mayapple is one of the first wild flowers to emerge from winter's icy grip. The Seneca people harvested the mayapple for its medicinal properties. It was a treatment for prostate, rheumatism and digestive disorders. Modern-day researchers are studying the mayapple's chemistry as a possible cancer treatment. Each plant will raise just one white flower, which by fall will produce a small fruit, a favorite food of the red fox.

Taking a sharp right turn, I leave the roadway and meet the blue trail, a dirt footpath that flanks two ridges thick with mature hemlock and the occasional oak. I hear the unmistakable *chip-churrr* of a scarlet tanager, recently arrived from its winter range in South America. Though common in this deciduous pine-oak forest, the vividly colored tanager is difficult to spot, preferring to perch, mostly motionless, in the canopy of the woods. I glass the treetops, but fail to spot the elusive caroler.

Bunches of purple-blue wild geraniums grace the forest floor. This perennial is also included in the native healer's herbal medicine chest. It was used to stop bleeding, and brewed as a tea to relieve the pain of toothache.

The trail drops a bit into a mix of hardwoods. A cluster of just-bloomed white dogwoods signal spring has at last arrived in these woods. I can hear the rush of Conklin Creek, tumbling some 120 feet over Angel Falls which lies up ahead.

Leaving the trail, I skirt a tangle of poison ivy and sit down on a fallen spruce. Its bark is blanketed with moss, thick and damp. No matter. From my wet perch I can see the sparkle of cascading water rushing over the rocks below.

Moss is nature's sponge, absorbing water when these woods are wet, giving it back when the woods dry. There are some 12,000 species of moss, which has spread over the earth's damp corners and crevasses for nearly half-a-billion years. The Seneca harvested its bounty for bedding, to dress wounds (moss has mild anti-bacterial properties) and to fill chinks between the logs of their longhouses.

A curious junco lands nearby. I hear a distant warbler, a single *peeep*. While I am less than an hour from downtown Rochester, the setting is reminiscent of the Adirondacks.

The pines that embrace me sing softly on a rising breeze. I close my eyes, disappearing into a wild and primitive fragrance that's floating around me.

○○

> "The finest workers in stone are not copper or steel tools, but the gentle touches of air and water working at their leisure with liberal allowances of time"
>
> — HDT, "A WEEK ON THE CONCORD AND MERRIMACK RIVERS"

Grimes Glen is not part of the High Tor Wildlife Management Area. Yet its proximity on the southerly edge of Naples village and three waterfalls (two of which drop more

Mark W. Holdren

than sixty feet) make Grimes Glen as magical a place as any in the western Finger Lakes region.

It is just after sunrise. The trailhead parking lot is empty of morning visitors. I am selfish; I want Grimes Glen all to myself. Changing into an old pair of sneakers, and with wading staff in hand, I head off. While I have come in late September, when the streams that feed the glen can be nearly bone dry, a week of steady rain will ensure the waterfalls will be in fine form.

Grimes Glen was created when melting headwaters at the end of last ice age scoured through multiple layers of sandstone, shale and limestone. The public has long enjoyed access, thankful to the generosity of its previous owner, and most recently through its purchase by the Finger Lakes Land Trust and subsequent transfer to Ontario County, which now manages Grimes Glen as a public park.

A footbridge leads to a wide trail that parallels the creek. The laborious groan of low-geared trucks climbing the steep roadway nearby is but a temporary annoyance. The disturbance is soon lost in the rush of water. The trees are a mix of hardwoods and hemlock. Dense colonies of ferns flourish in the damp shade, their delicate features, backlit in the morning sun, stand in stark contrast to the scabrous sheets of scraggy shale that seemingly dangle from the canyon walls.

Half-a-mile or so upstream I reach French Hills Falls. Here, Springstead Creek tumbles more than sixty feet to the floor of Grimes Glen. The sonorous thunder of water, rushing down the cliff side, the sparkle of morning light pirouetting through the cascade, the air, so fresh, so remarkably clean, all coalesce to clear my head of any infotoxins that may have hitched a ride with me this morning — my making the mistake earlier of listening to the morning news. If for no other reason, this is why we need nature; our level of happiness is determined by how we feel, not by what we know…or think we know.

Here the trail ends and I step cautiously in the stream. The walls of the canyon rise more than a hundred feet above me. Spindly maples sprout from shallow fissures in the rocks. Their ravenous roots are somehow able to draw sustenance from what little soil has found its way between miniscule cracks in the shale. The geological history of Grimes Glen lies bare before me. The fossil remains of ocean life found here — fish, sponges, jellyfish and clams — are a clear indication these rocks were created from the sediment of an ancient ocean. Grimes Glen is home to the Naples Tree, a 350-million-year-old tree fossil discovered there by local resident D. Dana Luther, in 1882. It now resides in the state museum in Albany.

A fallen hemlock lies partially submerged in the stream. It may one day achieve fossil fame. But this day it is simply a seat upon which I sit, enthralled by the raw symphony that plays out around me.

"A field of water betrays the spirit of the air," Thoreau wrote in *Walden*. "It is continually receiving new life and motion from above. It is intermediate in its nature between land and sky. On land only the grass and the trees wave. But the water itself is rippled by the wind. I see where the breeze dashes across it as streaks or flakes of light. It is unimaginable that we can look down on its surface. We shall perhaps look down thus on the surface of air and mark where a still subtler spirit sweeps over it."

Could Thoreau in 1854 have possibly imagined that a century later his contemporaries would gaze over Mother Earth from a perch nestled among the stars?

I wade upstream for about a quarter mile, reaching the second falls. Here the canyon walls narrow, forming a grotto of sorts. Its steep walls, carved from layers of limestone, sandstone and shale, are shrouded in a wispy mist. Of course I cannot taste or smell the magical molecules, the negative ions that swirl about me. But my mood is already brightened, a naturally induced euphoria triggered by increasing levels of serotonin in my bloodstream.

Remaining motionless, the rushing water washes my clumsy intrusion downstream. A red-bellied woodpecker resumes its *rat-a-tat* excavation of a long-dead maple. As the stream clears about my boots, a spiny crayfish emerges from hiding, crawling cautiously from beneath a mossy chunk of shale. These diminutive lobsters live only in the purest fresh water. Their presence here is an encouraging validation of the health of Grimes Creek.

The quality of this water is further confirmed when a school of fingerling rainbow trout passes by the tips of my boots. These are the lucky ones, so far. The females that spawned here in the spring deposited hundreds of thousands of eggs in nests, called redds, that they swatted from the gravelly streambed with their powerful tails.

These are the survivors, so far. They'll soon begin a perilous journey. Traveling from their birthplace to the marsh-like West River, they'll eventually reach the cool depths of Canandaigua Lake. But they must first pass through the West River, where a host of lethal predators — raccoons, mink and weasels, kingfishers and herons, snapping turtles and larger fish — lie in wait for them downstream.

Do these diminutive fish sense my trepidation? Do they somehow feel secure at my feet? Watching them float above the tips of my boots, my consciousness clears of every other thought but the present moment. Researchers say we humans have more than fifty thousand thoughts in a single day. And most of what rushes through our minds is negative. When we focus on a single thing, we unconsciously stop thinking. We create space between one thought and the next, thus short circuiting the flow of negative energy. Psychologists call this mindfulness, living solely in the present moment, where thinking is not required.

Immersing ourselves in nature surrounded by the very forces of our creation — we are able to reach a state of awareness not possible in our everyday lives.

> "I love Nature partly because she is not man, but a retreat from him. None of his institutions control or pervade her. There a different kind of right prevails. In her midst I can be glad with an entire gladness. If this world were all man, I could not stretch myself, I should lose all hope. He is constraint, she is freedom to me. He makes me wish for a different world. She makes me content with this."
> — HDT, *"Journal"*

WESLEY HILL NATURE PRESERVE

> "Art is not tame, and nature is not wild, in the ordinary sense. A perfect work of man's art would also be wild or natural in a good sense."
> — HDT, *"The Natural Man"*

If it were not for the vision of three artists, the diverse landscape that now encompasses the Wesley Hill Nature Preserve might easily have been lost to speculators whose ubiquitous and sprawling vacation home developments have clawed so deeply into the character of the Finger Lakes country.

John C. Wenrich and his friends James Havens and Colburn Dugan had longed for a place of "solitude and contemplation." Their search ended in 1926 when they purchased ninety acres of previously logged land east of Honeoye Lake.

The gem of their purchase was a portion of Briggs Gully, one of the largest in the Finger Lakes Region. The rolling hillside along the gorge's northern edge was rife with oak, white pine and maple seedlings. Soaring hemlocks, spared from the logger's saw, embraced the gorge's rim. Here they built a rudimentary cabin where the artists and their families nurtured the land — and their souls — for half a century. Thanks to their foresight and the stewardship of the Finger Lakes Land Trust, the former artists' retreat is not only protected from developers, but now includes an additional three hundred acres of surrounding hillside.

I have come here on a crisp autumn morning to do a little soul nurturing of my own. I've opted to explore the Red Rim Trail; it's one of five well-marked footpaths that rise and fall over the rolling terrain.

My arrival at the preserve's Gulick Road trailhead catches the attention of the keen-eyed gatekeeper, a jittery but ever vigilant red squirrel. Outraged by my presence, its furious chatter sounds the alarm.

Danger! Danger!

A wood thrush, whose flutelike notes — *eee-o-lay…eee-o-lay* — that had so cheered me moments ago, darts off into a thicket of wild grapes.

Serenade over.

Also heeding the squirrel's warning, a nearby woodpecker calls a halt to its rowdy work and disappears around the backside of a long dead ash tree.

Even the breeze has suddenly gone missing.

A disquieting stillness settles around me. My awkward arrival has clearly disturbed the natural order of things.

Oneness with nature begins with a slow pace and a soft footprint. The preserve's caretakers have wisely placed a wooden bench not far from the trailhead. Its purpose is clear: sit for a spell and allow the forest to awaken once again. Though the bench is yet damp with the morning's dew, I sit nonetheless. A little cold water on the behind will only sharpen my focus. I breathe deeply, once, twice, three times. My breath, like the stillness that surrounds me, is invisible. Deep invisible breathing creates space between our thoughts, clearing our consciousness of the worldly concerns we may have unwittingly brought to the forest with us.

The sweet, pungent scent of hemlock is everywhere. The smell of these eastern hemlocks — *Tsuga canadensis* — is similar to the poisonous parsnip family also called hemlock. While it was a lethal dose of *conium* (hemlock) that secured Socrates' death, the needles of these trees are not poisonous. Quite to the contrary, the Seneca people crushed them to brew an aromatic tea. And recently a popular perfume has been developed from an extract of oils from the black hemlock tree.

A century ago, the predecessors of these trees were cut and hauled to sawmills in Frosttown, a pioneer settlement adjacent to the nearby Cummings Nature Center. A small gauge rail line transported the milled logs down the steep hillside to the south end of Honeoye Lake. It was a perilous journey that once ended with the little engine and its cargo careening into the lake.

After loggers denuded the hillside, sheep farmers took a turn carving a living from the thin, rocky soil. Their efforts were short lived, however, and a new forest began to take root. Protected now from loggers and developers, these hemlocks face a new and equally dangerous threat — the sap-sucking woolly adelgid. These woods appear to be in good health, so far.

The breeze rises once more. Two playful chipmunks, head to tail, race past my feet, oblivious of my presence. A trio of black-capped chickadees flutters onto a nearby dogwood. In the distance I can hear that the woodpecker is back at work.

The forest has put my rude incursion aside.

Taking just a few steps at a time, heel first, rolling forward onto my toes, I proceed slowly and silently down the trail, which once served as a roadway to the Wenrich cabin. The forest transitions from soft-wood pine to maple and shagbark hickory. The trail is thick with acorn hulls. The squirrels and turkey here are living large. But there is a noticeable absence of oak seedlings. I suspect the burgeoning deer population. Disparagingly referred to as "hooved locusts" by many a frustrated gardener, whitetailed deer devour the tasty oak seedlings almost as soon as they sprout from the ground.

The rusted remains of a Model T Ford — a chunk of firewall and frame — lay in repose just off the trail. It's easy to imagine Wenrich and friends bouncing down the rutted road, their provisions in tow, eager for a long weekend in the woods.

At the half-mile mark, the nearly three-mile and mostly flat Red Rim Trail intersects with the shorter (0.7 mile) but more challenging Gully Trail. With a nod to Robert Frost, I choose the path less traveled and make my way down the steep slope to the floor of Brigg's Gully. This craggy, cavernous ravine was carved from mostly soft sedimentary rock by melting glacier water that rushed over this land at the end of the last ice age. Massive white pines and grand stands of oak embrace the precipitous trail, their roots having taken hold before the Civil War, and saved from the saw by the steep contour of the land.

There is a primordial aura to Brigg's Gully. It is a natural sanctuary where the forest bather can feel the unfathomable depth of nature and its connection to everything else. Nature is the path back to the source of our creation, a pathway to our true selves. I sit for a moment on a slab of shale. Water from a small feeder stream is rushing past me on its way to the valley below. As my breathing slows, the energy that is so discernible here flows freely around me. When we are one with nature, clarity returns to our life, which is surprisingly not as serious, complicated or as painful as our minds have made it out to be.

But Frost is nudging me on. I, too, have miles to go before I sleep. Climbing back to the top of the ridge, I mosey westerly among giant hemlocks and a stand of hardwoods that glitter in brilliant yellows, reds and oranges. The trail crosses another small stream. The sharp-eyed observer will spot a rusting pipe, about an inch in diameter, jutting from the stream bank. It's the handiwork of the owners of an early camp. Here they drew the icy water into the coils of a refrigerator in which they stored meats and other perishables. Pieces of the rusting coils are still visible. Like the remnants of the Model T, these traces of another era are slowly, relentlessly rotting away.

Marveling at the ingenuity of it all, I move on. But just ahead the trail falls off the edge of a deep gully. Fortunately, a thick rope has been provided to keep hikers from tumbling head first onto the rocks some 20 feet below. Though my rappelling skills are lacking, I make it safely to the gully floor and touch the very soul of Wesley Hill.

Here, all the elements that compose the diverse character of the preserve merge in surreal splendor: the melodic ripple of water over rock, the play of light through the treetops, and the piquant bouquet of damp leaves and rich black earth, all converge to create a place of peace, untouched by the human madness that rages around us.

Was Thoreau sitting in such a place when he wrote: "When I see the sun shining on the woods across the pond, I think this side the richer when I see it."

— HDT, *"Consciousness in Concord"*

I'm thankful to have this mystical, Eden-like setting all to myself.

But what's that?

Tucked into the stream bank, I spy an elf-sized structure of stones. The doorway is just four inches high. The windows are tiny, too. The roof is a slab of shale.

At first I credit its construction to human hands, a reader and admirer of *Grimm's Fairy Tales*, perhaps.

But what if…

Germanic mythology tells us that elves have magical powers and supernatural beauty. If so, here is surely where a band of merry gnomes would make their home.

Might their magic and the spiritual energy help me find clarity, relieving me from the madness that drives our frantic way of life?

Our minds are constantly generating what Buddha called *Dukkah*, which translates to *misery and unhappiness*. Only by living in the present moment can we free ourselves from the negativity that swirls around us. The present moment does not require thinking. Mindfulness is mindlessness. By listening only to the rush of the water, my consciousness clears of every random thought.

There is only now, the present moment.

But a noisy blue Jay breaks the spell.

Eeef! Eeef!

I grab hold of a second rope and climb back to the trail. It's just a short walk through an immense stand of red pine to the preserve's breathtaking overlook. Banks of billowy cumulous clouds drift like giant balls of cotton across a cobalt blue sky. The distant hills, bursting in autumn color, are untouched by the developer's blade. I suspect these hills appear much the same as they did to a Seneca hunter who must surely have passed here centuries ago.

"Wherever I go, I tread in the tracks of the Indian."

— HDT, *"Journal"*

I wonder if he, too, paused to admire the view. What burdens might he have carried with him… a lack of game, the hunger of his family, the coming of another harsh winter? Luck has spared me of these basic concerns, allowing me to connect with the natural world in a more cerebral manner.

The "Waldenesque" Wenrich cabin sits where the red and yellow trails intersect near the edge of Brigg's Gully. The cabin was built mostly of chestnut, and was completed shortly after the property was closed in 1927. A porch and kitchen were added some four years later. No more than 350 square feet or so, the cabin's knotted siding is gnarled and dark. A black snake of significant girth is lazily sunning itself on the warm shingles of the cabin's partially caved roof. The floor of the screened porch is in steady decay.

"Our mission is not to preserve buildings," the Finger Lakes Land Trust says.

It's clear from the deteriorating condition of the cabin that the trust is keeping its word.

I wonder what stories these weathered walls could tell?

But by thumbing through a pair of dog-eared notebooks that I've found on the porch, I'm able to listen to the voices of past cabin visitors:

> "What a magical discovery."
> "Annual journey of inspiration."
> "I got lost, but now I am found."
> "We found bear tracks."
> "God reveals himself in nature."

A child has scribbled the outline of a heart, and in it perhaps spoken for everyone who has visited the preserve:

> "This is a good place."

From the cabin's site, the trail climbs through both hemlock and hardwood. At first I'm serenaded by the *wee-see* of a black and white warbler, foraging for insects and larvae in the rotting trunk of a broken white pine. But it's a rowdy flock of red-wing blackbirds — *chuck...chuck...tee-ay* — that tell me the terrain is about to change.

The trail opens to rolling, sun-drenched meadow where

the fragrance of honeysuckle and Russian olive drift on the warm autumn breeze. The blackbirds I am hearing have gathered along the shoreline of a mirror-surfaced pond. It's surrounded with thick clusters of hawthorn and buttercups. At my approach, a portly bullfrog hops from the shoreline into the coal-black water. But the largemouth bass that are sunning themselves in the same shallows ignore my intrusion.

"In September or October, Walden is a perfect forest mirror, set round with stones as precious to my eyes as if fewer or rarer. Nothing so fair, so pure, and at the same time so large, as a lake, perchance lies on the surface of the earth."

— HDT *Walden*, "The Ponds"

Billowy cumulous clouds are floating in ominous shadows over the glassy surface of the pond. I've about made the "red trail loop." The Gulick Road trailhead, where my journey began, is just a short walk to the east. Once again, the preserve's wise caretakers have placed a bench just in the right place. This one overlooks the pond.

I sit for a spell. The warm sun is welcome after several hours in the damp woods, as is the perfume-rich fragrance of Russian olive — *Elaegnus angustifolia* — that grows so abundantly here. Despite its value in wildlife habitat, this native of western Asia has been designated an invasive species. Russian olive is able to fix nitrogen in its roots. It flourishes in the poorest of soils, thus easily overwhelming wild, native vegetation.

But Russian olive has its supporters. These include the cedar waxwings that are now gorging themselves on the plant's ripe, cherry-like berries. Native healers grind the fruit's dried powder, and mixing it with milk concocted a natural remedy for rheumatoid arthritis. Thus the debate rages on.

The red tailed hawk that's perched atop a dead maple at the edge of the woods is hungry, too. Its keen eyes sweep the meadow for a careless mouse or chipmunk. The *chicken hawk* — as it is despairingly referred to by some locals — is the most widely distributed hawk in North America. It is equally at home on the prairie, in woodlands or in the most populated cities where it feeds mostly on rats and pigeons. Because it is so easily trained, the red tail is the favorite of falconers world-wide. This bird's patience has apparently worn thin. Rising from its perch, it's soon hunting over a wider area, its wings beat deep and slow to conserve energy. Good hunting, my friend.

HEMLOCK & CANADICE LAKES WATERSHED

"My profession is to be always on the alert to find God in nature, to know his lurking places, to attend all the oratories, the operas in nature."

— HDT, *"Journal"*

"Glory! Hemlock Water at Last."

That was the headline in Rochester, New York, in January, 1876. The city's response to roiling epidemics of dysentery, cholera and typhoid was to tap the spring-pure water of Hemlock Lake for the city's drinking water. This would initiate a near century-and-a-half effort to protect the

39,000-acre Hemlock-Canadice lakes watershed.

The wild, unspoiled shorelines of both lakes and the undeveloped hillsides embracing them are unique in all the Finger Lakes. Here, the forest bather's senses open to an aria composed by nature in notes of water and light, sounds and smells.

The maestro responsible for creating this open air opera house was the project's chief engineer, Nelson Tubbs. A man with a "flair for showmanship and immune from political barbs," he completed the nearly twenty-nine mile, gravity-fed pipeline from Hemlock Lake to Rochester in less than three years. In 1919, some forty-three years later, nearby Canadice Lake was connected to the Hemlock line via a five-foot diameter pipe. This increased the flow of fresh drinking water into Rochester by twenty-five percent.

To help ensure the purity of the lakes' drinking water, the city of Rochester began buying up lake shore property in 1895. By 1950, every cabin, summer home and hotel had been demolished.

The watershed was carefully managed by the city. Swimming was prohibited. Boaters were required to obtain permits. The use of outboard motors was restricted to ten horsepower and boat lengths to no more than seventeen feet.

These restrictions protected the lake's purity for more

than a century. In the 1950s Rochester's Genesee Brewing Company anchored its advertising campaign with the slogan "Brewed with pure Hemlock Lake water."

Development pressures continued to escalate across the Finger Lakes. By the 1990s the cash-strapped city of Rochester (now relying more heavily on water from Lake Ontario) began to explore the sale of its increasingly valuable Hemlock and Canadice real estate. A joint effort to preserve this natural legacy was launched by the Finger Lakes Land Trust and the Nature Conservancy. Their efforts culminated in 2010 with New York State's purchase of the city's watershed holdings. The 6,684-acre Hemlock-Canadice State Forest is now managed and protected by the state's Department of Environmental Conservation.

It is early May. The hardwoods that hug the Canadice shoreline are a wash of light yellows and pale greens. My morning mosey begins just off the Canadice Lake Road at the southern tip of the lake. A three-mile plus trail begins here. It crosses the lake's rich wetlands, and then parallels the western shore of the lake, terminating at Purcell Hill Road at the north end of the lake.

Though a tranquil stillness lies over the land, new life is bursting forth about me. Skunk or swamp cabbage thrives in the water-soaked bog on either side of the trail. Native to eastern North America, skunk cabbage is an early spring arrival. Through a process called cellular respiration, this plant is able to generate its own heat — up to 60 degrees — and push its way to the forest surface through ground still locked in winter's grasp. Its ample green leaves, up to twenty inches long and fifteen inches wide, give off a pungent odor, attractive to stone flies and bees, but repugnant to most animals. But when dried, the leaves were used by the Seneca in soups and stews.

I startle a pair of mallards that beat a hasty retreat up the lake. An observation area has been cleared along the marsh trail. The view is northerly, taking in a wide sweep of the lake and adjacent hills. I am just thirty miles from the city of Rochester, but the stunning panorama unfolding before me could be in the heart of the Adirondack Park.

While the breeze is still, the morning songs of birds — chickadees, warblers and wrens — reverberate from the woodlands around me.

> "As I come over the hill, I hear the wood thrush singing…This is the only bird whose notes affect me like music, affect the flow and tenor of my thought, my fancy and imagination. It lifts and exhilarates me. It is a medicative draught to my soul. It changes

> all hours to an eternal morning. It banishes all trivialness. It reinstates me in my dominion, makes me the lord of creation, the chief musician to my court. This minstrel sings in time, a heroic age, with which no event in the village can be contemporary."
>
> — HDT, *"Journal"*

The morning sun pleases a nearby Baltimore oriole. Its flute-like whistle has caught my ear, its vivid orange breast my eye. I wonder did it winter in Mexico, or did it migrate even further, from South America, perhaps? The ability of small birds weighing mere ounces to fly such staggering distances — not just once but twice each year — is incomprehensible to me.

The warm, marsh-like shallows of the lake teem with carp, foraging just beneath the surface, oblivious to the danger that is circling above them. The bald eagle has no doubt spotted me as well. But I am not the focus of its attention. It has other fish to fry, so to speak.

The bald eagle was not a unanimous choice as our national symbol. Ben Franklin opposed it, noting the eagle's habit of stealing prey from lesser birds. Franklin's favorite was the turkey. Fortunately, wiser heads prevailed.

Hunters and the widespread use of the chemical DDT

to control mosquitoes and black flies pretty much wiped the bald eagle from the American landscape. But following the banning of the lethal pesticide in 1972 and the addition of the bald eagle to the Endangered Species Act a year later, the bald eagle has made a remarkable comeback. These most regal of birds are now sighted across the Finger Lakes region.

With its wingspan of nearly seven feet, the eagle I am watching can climb to 10,000 feet and dive toward its prey at sixty miles per hour. But for now my eagle appears content just admiring the view. The carp wallowing in the weeds are safe…for the time being. While I have delighted in the view as well, it is time move on.

The trail ahead is bordered with thickets of Russian olive and stands of swamp maple. The decaying carcass of what was once a Ford Falcon lies almost hidden in the high grass. Here the trail turns north, following a course which once was known as the Canadice Haul Road. Here and there, moss-draped concrete footers, fallen stone walls, and the occasional rusted oil can are the last remnants of the cottages and hotels that once dominated the waterfront.

Canadice is the smallest of the Finger Lakes, just three miles long. But its elevation of 1,096 feet makes it the highest of its six sister lakes. With a maximum depth of 90 feet, Canadice holds a healthy population of lake, rainbow and brown trout. Pickerel, yellow perch and smallmouth bass flourish in the lake's warmer levels.

Wetland vegetation soon yields to a woodland habitat. Evidence of the lake's glacial origin is scattered about me in the form of glacial erratics — giant-sized boulders left behind as the mile-thick ice that carved the Finger Lakes landscape receded north at the end of the last ice age.

The trail rises along the ridgeline. Beneath a cobalt-blue sky, the lake shimmers like a field of gleaming diamonds. A lone fisherman in a small wood boat drifts by. He's trolling for trout, no doubt, along the edge of the drop off that I know lies about 50 yards or so offshore. I fished here with my father, now more than half a century ago. Our boat was my father's first, an 8-foot plywood dingy that he built one winter in our basement. I wondered as he sawed, sanded and glued if it would fit through doors when completed.

It did, by an inch or so.

Though the little boat was easily transported on the roof of our 1955 Plymouth Belvedere, most of the time my father just "stored it" along the lakeshore, chained to a tree. This was the practice of the day, and the city of Rochester did not seem to mind. Some boats were left behind, their rotting remains scattered here and there along the shoreline.

Bigger boats would follow for my father. He fished

mostly on Seneca Lake. He was well equipped with a fish finder, depth finder, deep trolling rigs, a two-way radio and enough spoons, lures, lines and hooks to stock a tackle shop. We caught more fish, but the lazy joy of watching a red and white plastic bobber ride the water from a little wooden boat was lost forever.

Deep in the forest, a woodpecker is hard at work. At first I think it a pileated woodpecker. But the beats are sporadic. A pileated woodpecker's are steady.

A red-headed woodpecker, I wonder.

I glass the trees. The red-headed woodpecker is a rare bird in these parts, sometimes vanishing for years. The tapping stops. My binoculars fill with nothing but leaves.

What I do see, scattered about the trail, are the remains — nothing more than a few blue and white feathers — of an ill-fated blue jay. The handy work of an owl or hawk, no doubt.

The trail is bordered with dense clusters of purple-blue periwinkle, popular among gardeners as a ground cover. I'm betting these are the descendants of plants that long ago graced the garden of a Canadice cottage owner. While periwinkle thrives in the deep shade, wild cherry is flourishing along the sun-drenched shoreline, their buds bursting with dazzling white flowers.

Water that's seeping from countless hillside springs has gathered in shallow pools along the edge of the trail, nurturing yellow clusters of St. Johnswort. Further along, the trailside is generously sprinkled with purple geraniums, wild mustard, purple-blue and white shaped asters, and brambles of blackberry.

But my eyes are drawn to a dense spray of white trillium. Kneeling onto the moist earth, I run my fingers over this woodland perennial's soft, three-petaled flowers. The Buddha is said to have given a silent sermon in which he held up a flower. He simply gazed at it. After a while, a monk named Mahakasyapa smiled. He was the only one who "got it." The Buddha's point was that flowers are messengers from another realm and are able to awaken humans to the beauty of our truest nature. Thoreau clearly "got it," writing of the fragrance of flowers, "They who scent it can never faint." So I linger for a moment, bathing in the miracle that is spring.

Beneath a stand of giant hemlocks the remains of a stone fireplace juts from the weeds, evidence of the lake's boom times. A set of concrete steps leads to the lakeshore. It is bordered with yellow daffodils in full bloom. I wonder what sort of structure sat here. Who were the families that enjoyed this view of the lake from the porch of their summer cottage?

A Spandex-clad jogger, with a lumbering, black retriever

in tow, crosses my path. We exchange hellos and she is gone. Once again I have these woods to myself. I make for a dense plot of hemlock and white pine that stands between the trail and the shore of the lake. Here, the forest bather can remain unseen from intruders on the trail. While the gentle fragrance of these evergreens is not overwhelming, its subtle bouquet may have inspired Thoreau, who believed that trees were full of poetry, and pines impressed him as human.

> "The trees indeed have hearts. With certain affection the sun seems to send its farewell ray far and level over the copes of them, and they silently receive it with gratitude, like a group of settlers with their children."
> — HDT, *"Journal"*

A loon pops to the surface of the lake. Its white necklace and cheeks flash in the sun. It's joined by its mate, who surfaces some twenty yards down shore. I wonder if these loons are just passing through on their way north to the Adirondacks, perhaps, or further on to Canada. Or have they decided to nest here. Loons are monogamous and bond for up to five years.

I hope they stay.

Perhaps no sound in nature defines the call of the wild

as when the waters ring with the loon's wild laughter. The presence of loons here is indicative of the high quality of Canadice Lake water. Loons require clear water in which to see their prey. Unlike most birds, a loon's bones are not hollow, thus reducing their buoyancy, making them efficient divers. Underwater, loons chase down their prey, mostly small perch and bluegills, swallowing them whole. A pair of adult loons and their chicks can consume half a ton of fish in a single summer. While they are awkward on the ground, loons can fly up to seventy miles per hour. But an errant landing can be fatal. Loons sometimes mistake water-covered parking lots for a lake, or will land on ponds too small; loons can require up to a quarter mile of water to achieve liftoff.

These Canadice loons will leave for their winter quarters along the southeast coast of America in October. I am hoping they will nest successfully. If so, the adults will depart first. The youngsters will have to make it on their own, leaving a few weeks later. The juveniles, mostly black in color, will remain in the south for two years, flying north to breed in their third year.

This pair hoots softly to one another. It's their way of keeping in contact. The loon's eerie call is one of the most spellbinding in all of nature. The writer John McPhee called it "the laugh of the deeply insane." The loon's tremolo call announces its presence; the yodel is a territorial claim that changes when a loon relocates to a new territory, and the haunting wail is when loons attempt to locate each other.

> "This is the loon — I don't mean its laugh, but its looning — is a long drawn call, as it were, sometimes singularly human to my ear-hoo-hooooo, like the hallowing of a man on very high key, having thrown his voice into his head. I have heard a sound exactly like it when breathing heavily through my nostrils half awake at ten at night, suggesting my affinity to the loon, as if its language were but a dialect of my own…"
>
> — HDT, *"The Maine Woods"*

The Canadice haul trail is as enchanting in winter as any other season. The constantly changing play of light and shadow create a mystical dimension in which the forest bather — on cross-country skis or snowshoes — can experience nature in its starkest terms. The absence of foliage widens the view, showcasing the rise and fall of the land. Fresh snow reveals the comings and goings of the red fox and hare, the mouse and the whitetailed deer. With due respect to Robert Service, the silence of a woods in winter does not "bludgeon you dumb." Quite the opposite is true. A still winter's day opens the forest bather's senses to the very spirit of renewal.

> "The finest winter day is a cold but clear and glittering one. There is a remarkable life in the air then, and birds and other creatures appear to feel it, to be excited and invigorated by it."
> — HDT, "*Journal*"

The myth that the Inuit people have hundreds of words for snow has long been dispelled. They have two: the noun, *aput*, and the verb, *qannig*. The snow watchers at Cal Tech, however, have identified 35 distinct snowflake types, from prisms to plates, fern-like dendrites, needles, cups, sheaths, triangle bullets and columns. All are visible to the winter forest bather with the aid of a pocket-sized magnifying glass.

The biologist and theorist E.O. Wilson in his book, *The Creation*, coined the term "micro-wilderness" — a biosphere of micro inhabitants that includes algae and fungi, mites, insects and other arthropods that flourish under our feet, mostly invisible to the naked eye.

Adding perspective, Wilson wrote: "For an oribatid mite, a rotting tree stump is the equivalent of Manhattan."

Thoreau & Me

HARRIET HOLLISTER SPENCER STATE RECREATION AREA

The wind has many voices. There is no better place to listen than at the Harriet-Hollister Spencer State Recreation Area. Tucked atop the steep hill country separating Canadice and Honeoye lakes, this diverse woodland offers the forest bather not only solitude, but a breathtaking view of the Honeoye Lake watershed as well.

There is a threatening hue to the cumulous clouds rising over the lake. While these cotton-like clouds hold little or no moisture, they are often forerunners of their more potent brethren, the power-backed cumulonimbus, which often accompany severe storms.

"The most beautiful thing in nature is the sun reflected from a tearful cloud." — HDT, *"Journal"*

While the sun is dancing through the leaves overhead, there is a cold rush to the wind that is gathering strength behind me. Spotting a weathered bench just off the park's access road, I sit for a spell.

There is a small plaque informing me this was "The Favorite Place of Todd Ewers." The reason why is immediately clear. The view overlooking Honeoye Lake and the gentle hills beyond is spectacular.

I have ten miles of trails, with names like Big Oak, Bear Cub and Raccoon, from which to make my morning ramble. With one of the higher elevations in the Finger Lakes, Harriet Hollister is among the first to record heavy snowfalls. In winter, these trails attract cross-country skiers from across the region.

The woods where I start off are mostly white pine. There is a sprinkle of spruce, and red and striped maple, a tree whose green striped bark gives it the look of a plant more than a tree. There is enough light sifting through the leafy canopy to encourage a new generation of spruce. Their seedlings are scattered about the forest floor, popping up through dense clusters of featherlike ferns.

A red-eyed vireo — *here I am...where are you* — sings out to me, but I cannot see it through the foliage. These woods are filled with an incredible variety of songbirds. In just a quarter mile or so I spot a Parula warbler, a red-breasted nuthatch, a flock of robins, a rose-breasted grosbeak, a flock of jittery juncos, a black-throated warbler and a yellow-bellied sapsucker.

> "I once had a sparrow alight upon my shoulder for a moment...and I felt that I was more distinguished by that circumstance than I should have been by any epaulet I could have worn."
> — HDT, "*Journal*"

A tiger swallowtail butterfly takes up my company, escorting me from the pines and into a stand of maple and ash. Here and there the forest floor is bathed in soft sun. Pink and white trillium, wild geraniums and violets, Canada mayflowers, their leaves not yet blossomed, and purple-fringed polygala are busting forth on both sides of the trail.

But these woodlands soon transition to open meadow. A covey of little wood satyrs flutters about in the tall grass. These chestnut brown butterflies are easy to identify. The dark eye spots surrounded by yellow on their wings quickly gives them away.

A blue bird catches my eye, then another.

"The bluebird carries the sky on its back."

— HDT, *"Journal"*

Bluebirds are territorial, and prefer open grasslands. Their numbers had declined significantly by the 1970s. Nonnative sparrows and starlings often drive bluebirds from their nests, smashing incubating eggs and sometimes killing the adults. But thanks to the efforts of volunteers who build and maintain nesting boxes placed along bluebird trails, these brightly colored birds are making a comeback. Gardeners are particularly fond of bluebirds. They are voracious insect eaters. The bluebird's rich warble has long been an inspiration for songwriters: from Jan Peerce's "Bluebird of happiness" to David Bowie's "Lazarus". Bowie found the bluebird a metaphor for life after death. And of course there is "Zip-a-Dee-Dodah" or Mr. Bluebird on My Shoulder.

The trail has taken me full circle. I've returned to the Honeoye Lake overlook. Though countless cottages and summer homes seemingly rim every inch of the lakeshore, the surrounding panorama is pretty much untouched by human hands. I came to Harriet Hollister this morning to bathe in spring's eternal energy. But it's the wind, nature's very breath, that has taken hold of me.

The wind has long served writers and poets as a metaphor for change. In nature, shifts in the wind's direction and velocity are sure harbingers that the weather is about to change. The wind can also sweep from our minds all that stuff that accumulates inside us, if we take the time to listen.

The story is told of two Zen monks, Ekido and Tanzan, walking a muddy, rain-drenched road. They came upon a young woman trying to cross, but the water was too deep. Tanzan picked her up and carried her to the other side. The pair walked on in silence for several hours. Ekido, unable to restrain himself any longer, finally asked: "Why did you carry that girl across the road? We monks are not supposed to do things like that."

"I put the girl down hours ago," Tanzan replied. "Are you still carrying her?"

Imagine how enlightened our lives could be if we simply let go, of the burdens — mostly imaginary — that we lug around with us every day. The wind can sweep the past clean, awakening us to what the writer Eckhart Tolle called "the Power of Now."

Now is all there is.

Mark W. Holdren

THE FINGER LAKES NATIONAL FOREST

One begins to sense the grandeur of the Finger Lakes National Forest long before setting foot on one of its thirty miles of interconnecting trails. I am driving south on Route 414. Seneca Lake shimmers to the west; unbroken woodlands embrace Backbone Ridge, that separates Seneca and Cayuga lakes. Stretching more than ten miles between the lakes, the Finger Lakes National Forest features more than 16,000 acres of diverse forest, meadow and wetland habitat.

European settlers began farming this region of the

Finger Lakes at the conclusion of the Revolutionary War. Most prospered until the Great Depression. That's when the Federal Government began encouraging farmers to re-settle where greater employment opportunities could be found. Between 1938 and 1941 more than one hundred farms were bought up by the Federal Soil Conservation Service, which then managed the land as the Hector Land Use Area. Its task was to stabilize the soil and convert its use from crops to livestock. Ten years into that effort, increased efforts were placed on multi-use management. In 1983 responsibility for the land was handed off to the National Forest System. It was formally dedicated the Finger Lakes National Forest in 1985. It is unique among most public land areas as it is managed for recreation, livestock grazing, wildlife habitat preservation and timber harvesting, truly a multi-use area.

The transition from farm to forest begins as soon as I leave Route 414 and climb the ridge via Mathews Road. Asphalt grudgingly gives way to gravel. Tidy farms and manicured gardens and landscapes fade away in my rear-view mirror.

Mathews Road meets Burnt Hill Road near the crest of the ridge. I hang a right, and I'm in luck. The Burnt Hill trailhead parking lot is unoccupied. It is early September. The maples that embrace the trailhead have not yet begun to display their royal luster.

I take a moment to pick up half a dozen empty Budweiser cans and toss them in my car. The visitors who preceded me here clearly had little respect for the wonders that surrounded them.

The Burnt Hill Trail crosses a sun-dappled meadow thick with white asters and purple knapweed. A bobolink is fluttering about over the tall grass. Its voice has a banjo-like quality — *bobolink...bobolink...bobolink.* This male, with its distinctive golden buff nape, whitish scapulars and wide, flattish tail, will soon be off to its winter quarters in South America. I'm fortunate to have seen it. The bobolink's numbers are in steady decline across the northeast.

Minutes into my mosey, I've reached Gorge Ponds, two small but nonetheless enchanting droplets upon the earth. I wish I'd brought my folding chair. I could easily spend my day here, marveling at the acrobatic swallows that are skimming water for emerging flies, and watching the ponds change the moods in the shifting light.

Thoreau on Walden Pond:

"It is a mirror which no stone can crack, whose quicksilver will never wear off, whose gilding nature continually repairs; no storm no dust can dim its surface ever fresh."

But I must move on.

Thoreau & Me

The trail leaves the meadow and winds through a pocket of hardwoods. A blue jay cries out from a treetop. I could walk the trail eyes closed and the songs of birds would tell me upon what terrain I passed. Marsh ferns blanket the forest floor, nurtured by countless springs seeping down the hillside.

A giant fallen oak, like a beached whale, lies just off the trail. Its once nearly impenetrable bark is rotting and cloaked in thick moss. Was it a lightning strike that took it to the ground? Or did it simply grow weary with age and tumble from its lofty place among the trees? When did it spring from this ground as a seedling? Putting on my dendrochronologist's hat — the science of tree dating — I count its growth rings and determine this once mighty oak grew for more than a century. I wonder what it saw, who and what may have passed beneath its once lofty limbs.

I cross a dry streambed, then another. Maple, beech and hickory give way to pine. The sun slips behind the clouds, and the woods suddenly grow colder. The gorge is now in view, but what in the devil is that? Just to my right lies a serpent shaped pile of rocks. Perhaps thirty feet in length, it twists like a snake down toward the gorge. Was it once a stone wall? Did the ground shift, a tremor perhaps, and re-arrange the wall builder's work? One thing is clear: these stones were placed here by the hand of man.

The fallen oak... The old stone wall... one long dead, the other twisted and torn. The birds have suddenly gone silent. The passing clouds are casting long, finger-like shadows through the trees. But at the edge of the gorge a single shaft of sunlight shines brightly on a wide, flat stone. Its silken surface is welcoming and warm.

I think I will sit here for a while.

Thoreau & Me

Mark W. Holdren

CONCLUSION

What might Thoreau have seen if he'd ambled across the Finger Lakes country? Would he have waxed as poetically over High Tor and Canadice Lake as he did over Walden Pond or the Merrimack?

Yes, I believe he would have.

Thoreau left us innumerable lessons in the "art of living well." He taught us that nature was a place of reverence and awe, not some obstacle to be conquered and restrained. "Be always on the alert to find God in nature."

He believed we do best when we are most ourselves. We must "live deep and suck all the marrow out of life." Silence and solitude were not to be feared, but embraced. "Silence alone is worthy to be heard."

One of America's first and finest nature writers, Henry David Thoreau's work helps us to better understand our relationship with the natural world. His view was clearly through all of his senses. He heard beyond the range of sound. He saw beyond the range of light.

"Live in each season as it passes; breathe the air, drink the drink, taste the fruit, and resign yourself to the

> influence of each…Be blown on by all the winds. Open all your pours and bathe in all the tides of nature, in all her streams and oceans, all seasons…Grow green with spring, yellow and ripe with autumn. Drink of each season's influence as a vial, a true panacea of all remedies mixed for your especial use."
>
> — HDT, *"Journal"*

There can be little doubt that Thoreau's work, if not the foundation of the practice of shinrin-yoku, has inspired its growth throughout the world.

What Thoreau wrote so poetically of the therapeutic powers of nature has now been proven by scientific studies. The same forces that give life to plants can be transferred to humans, thus improving our well-being. The natural world is forever embedded in our genes. We don't need scientists to tell us we simply feel better in nature than we do when confined to artificial man-made environments.

Nature is the path back to our true selves. Everything in nature has unfathomable depth. As depth returns to our lives, our awareness grows. Awareness is the power concealed in the present moment, where our minds clear and our senses open to all the wonders of life.

While my connection to the places of which I have

written is powerful and life-sustaining, you are free to discover your own sacred places, for they abound throughout the Finger Lakes country.

Thoreau believed we grow through self-realization, a process by which we unfold new layers of awareness through contact with our real self, what he called "the perennial source of our life."

And the source of all life is the natural world, where Thoreau wrote that the sun would shine into our minds and hearts and "light our whole lives with a great awakening light."

While Thoreau never sauntered through the Finger Lakes country, we can feel his presence whenever we go forth to be one with the land.

"I learned this, at least, by my experiment; that if one advances confidently in the direction of his dreams, and endeavors to live the life in which he has imagined, he will meet with a success unexpected in common hours; He will put some things behind, will pass an invisible boundary; new, more universal laws will begin to establish themselves in and around him; old laws will be expanded and interpreted in his favor in a more liberal sense, and he will live with the license of a higher order of beings."

— HDT, *Walden* "Conclusion"

CPSIA
Printed i
BVOW08
460113

Information can be obtained at www.ICGtesting.com
the USA
0929290816
BV00001B/3/P